OCCULT
GRANDMASTERS
EXPOSED

Dangerous Spiritual Warfare Prayers and Decrees
to Stop Witches & Wizards in Their Tracks

WRITTEN BY
JOSEPH C. OKAFOR

Your Thank You Gift

As a token of gratitude for your purchase *Occult Grand Masters Exposed*, I am pleased to present you with both the book *"Commanding Your Dominion"* and the course *"Blueprint to Overcome Hatred & Rejection"* as a complimentary gift.

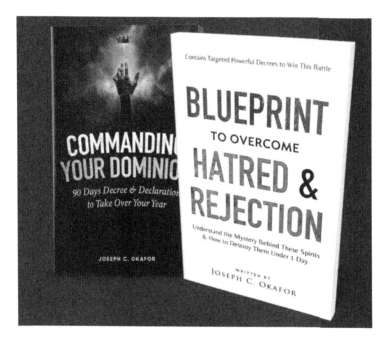

Please follow the link provided below, or enter the URL directly into your browser ↓

cojoseph.com

CONTENTS

CHAPTER ONE

The Supreme Authority of Occultism

In the proper context, one could argue that occultism is nothing more than a secret gathering of some people who are bound by an oath or certain conditions to invoke or perpetrate an agenda, usually a demonic agenda of dominion and subjugation, as opposed to the divine mandate God gave to Adam and Eve, and by extension, to all humans, to subdue it: They rule over all the creatures that swim the seas, the birds in the sky, and the livestock on the land.

The main issue is that some humans, inspired by Lucifer and his host of demons, seek more. They desire total subjugation and domination over their fellow humans, as well as complete control over the affairs of all males they regard as less intelligent regular mortals. This runs counter to God's holy duty to man to tame and rule over all animals. However, some humans want the mandate extended to humans they consider less enlightened and ordinary, and this is the hidden goal of occultism.

Satan is the primary spirit at work in occultism. Remember how Satan tricked Eve by telling her that if she ate the forbidden fruit, she would not die. For God knows that the day you eat thereof, your eyes shall be opened, and you shall be as gods, understanding good and evil' (Genesis 3:4-5). Would you expect the devil to abandon man after the fall? Wrong! Lucifer has long constructed castles and numerous abodes in the hearts of humanity. He has complete command over men. Those who adore him congregate in secret places. They engage in occult rituals and spirit worship.. They try to recruit as many men and women as possible. The expansionist theory is never-ending.

Globally, occultism is commonplace, with numerous dimensions and orders, many of which are known and many of which are mysterious. The imposition of a rule of secrecy and death penalties for violating the cult's codes are two characteristics that all occult societies have in common.

It is nearly impossible to agree on whether there is such a thing as a good occult group because many religious establishments, both past and present, have been at the forefront of occultism all in the name of worshipping one deity or another. There is a fine line between good and evil. But the truth is that good will never be evil, and evil will never be good. Light will never become darkness, and darkness will never become light. It is (and always will be) one of two things: light or darkness, good or evil.

What Exactly Is Occultism?

Occultism is a diabolical endeavour that is hidden from public view. It is the devil's activities that are mostly unknown to members of occult organisations. Occultism, which centres around wicked operations not easily perceived or understood by none members, is only practiced by those in covenant with Satan. Occultism is obscure, secretive, and off-limits to the general public. In most circumstances, clinical tools cannot detect the operations of the shadow world.

Occultism is the evil involvement with supernatural abilities or knowledge of the devil. It is a malicious action or influence of supernatural or supernormal forces intended to destroy lives and property. An occultist seeks power, information, or assistance from malevolent spirits. They sacrifice to the devil, practice divination, and employ charms and enchantments.

The antichrist, Satan, is the ruler of occultism and demonic intelligence. The devil is currently destroying the globe through occultism. Combining spiritual intelligence with occult rituals is harmful. With occultism, which causes individuals to be selfish, evil, irrational, cruel, and thoughtless, no nation will flourish or remain progressive. When faced with defeat, occult people become nasty, suicidal, and insane, as was the case in Babylon.

"For this cause the king was angry and very furious, and commanded to destroy all the wise men of Babylon. And the decree went forth that the wise men should be slain;

4

and they sought Daniel and his fellows to be slain" (Daniel 2:12-13).

Knowledge without a genuine relationship with God is incompatible with the spirit of country building. No one can be an occultist and still have a relationship with God because occultism kills genuine knowledge over time. Genuine knowledge and intelligence come from God, and when benefactors refuse to devote their lives to God, their knowledge and intelligence are corrupted and reduced to vanity (see Ezekiel 28:1-19; Psalms 39:5). As a result, while Satan is the father of occultism and witchcraft, the queen of heaven is its mother.

CHAPTER TWO

Occult and Magic Practices in The Home

S aul, from the tribe of Benjamin, was the first King of Israel. He was a charming, good-looking young man who was better than all the other young men in Israel. From the top of his neck up, he was taller than other people. In the Bible, Saul is described in beautiful ways.

"And he had a son, whose name was Saul, a choice young man, and a goodly: and there was not among the children of Israel a goodlier person than he: from his shoulders and upward he was higher than any of the people" (1 Samuel 9:2).

"And they ran and fetched him thence: and when he stood among the people, he was higher than any of the people from his shoulders and upward" (1 Samuel 10:23).

He began as a humble and God-fearing man who revered God's servants, and God directed Samuel to anoint Saul as King of Israel (see 1 Samuel 9:15-27). Saul remained devoted to his father, Kish. He was on his way to find his father's missing asses when he met the greatest God's servant of his time. Saul was allowed to dine with the prophet in the chief's place among thirty people, and he was anointed as King and commissioned to rule God's children. Saul stated in the book of 1 Samuel 9:21;

"Am not I a Benjamite, of the smallest of the tribes of Israel? and my family the least of all the families of the tribe of Benjamin? Wherefore then speakest thou so to me?" (1 Samuel 9:21).

God recognized him by his name, family name, and tribe. That is why God gave him particular instructions on his role as King. Saul was separated for a divine purpose. He was particularly summoned and anointed for this reason.

He got a new heart, prophesied with other prophets, and was commissioned to reign over Israel after being filled with the Spirit of God. He guarded Israel's children, battled and defeated the Ammonites, and was confirmed and widely acclaimed as King by the entire nation.

Through his impatience and disobedience to God's particular mandate, Saul indoctrinated his family into occultism and witchcraft. Instead of repenting and seeking God's forgiveness, as David would later demonstrate, Saul refused to accept responsibility for his mistakes. He battled with God and blamed others. He was afraid of the unknown, so he did foolish things instead of repenting, confessing, and abandoning his wrongdoing. Gospel ministers must be aware of this if they are to live to fulfil their ministries and destinies.

"And Samuel said to Saul, thou hast done foolishly: thou hast not kept the commandment of the Lord thy God, which he commanded thee: for now, would the Lord have established thy kingdom upon Israel forever. But now thy

kingdom shall not continue: the Lord hath sought him a man after his own heart, and the Lord hath commanded him to be captain over his people, because thou hast not kept that which the Lord commanded thee. And Samuel arose, and gat him up from Gilgal unto Gibeah of Benjamin. And Saul numbered the people that were present with him, about six hundred men" (1 Samuel 13:13-15).

Surprisingly, after Samuel's sentence on him, his family, and the throne, one would expect Saul to feel some sorrow. But Saul remained unaffected. Samuel detailed Saul's faults, chastised him for his foolish conduct and disobedience to God's word, and thereby deposed him as King. Nonetheless, Saul showed no remorse or hint of contrition. He let Samuel go without resolving any issues with him or God. Instead, Saul counted the people with him and marched to war with the Philistines, disregarding Samuel's edict and never returning to ask for his assistance.

Despite his lack of repentance, God granted him victory over his foes by His mercies and kindness. There is a principle at work here: obtaining victory after blatant disobedience, doing exploits by praying and receiving answers to your prayers, and rising material prosperity in sin and disobedience to God's Word do not imply God's permission for you to stay in sin. It's only a matter of time before you realize it was all God's grace all along.

"Then Saul went up from following the Philistines: and the Philistines went to their own place. So, Saul took the kingdom over Israel, and fought against all his enemies on every side, against Moab, and against the children of Ammon, and against Edom, and against the kings of Zobah, and against the Philistines: and whithersoever he turned himself, he vexed them. And he gathered a host, and smote the Amalekites, and delivered Israel out of the hands of them that spoiled them" (1 Samuel 14:46-48).

Many family, community, and church leaders have knowingly defied God's commandments and regulations, committed immorality, and are guilty of all types of sin, yet they are economically prosperous in whatever they do. This was true of King Saul. Prosperity in sin is a huge deception and witchcraft occult manipulation. When you sin and fail to repent, the devil will plant seeds of witchcraft, cravings for transitory rewards over relationship with God, and prosperity and victory without purity in you. He will turn your heart to live unrighteously until you are removed from God's presence. If you observe someone succeeding and enjoying life while living in sin, do not idolize them in any manner because they may be on their way to witchcraft bondage.

"Samuel also said unto Saul, The Lord sent me to anoint thee to be king over his people, over Israel: now therefore hearken thou unto the voice of the words of the Lord. Thus, saith the Lord of hosts, I remember that which Amalek did to Israel, how he laid wait for him in the way, when he

came up from Egypt. Now go and smite Amalek, and

utterly destroy all that they have, and spare them not; but

slay both man and woman, infant and suckling, ox and

sheep, camel and ass" (1 Samuel 15:1-3).

Do you comprehend that despite Saul's atrocities, God sent Samuel to him for other purposes in His favour and mercy? What does that imply? Occupying or keeping divine position after committing sin without sincere repentance does not imply that you are in good standing with God. Receiving prophecies or hearing God's Word while living in sin is also not proof that you are a child of God. You make a mockery of your calling and anointing if you remain in your sins. As long as sin reigns supreme in your life, winning a battle or gaining answers to your prayers as a sinner does not imply that God is pleased with you. Healing the sick, delivering prisoners, casting out demons, and defeating your enemies while still sinful are not guarantees that God is with you.

"And Saul gathered the people together, and numbered them in Telaim, two hundred thousand footmen, and ten thousand men of Judah. And Saul came to a city of Amalek, and laid wait in the valley. And Saul said unto the Kenites, Go, depart, get you down from among the Amalekites, lest I destroy you with them: for ye shewed kindness to all the children of Israel, when they came up out of Egypt. So, the Kenites departed from among the Amalekites. And Saul smote the Amalekites from Havilah until thou comest to Shur, that is over against Egypt. And he took Agag the king of the Amalekites alive, and utterly destroyed all the people with the edge of the sword" (1 Samuel 15:4-8).

Saul's spiritual throne ended, although he remained physically king. Samuel was sent by God to offer him a second chance to hear and obey God's Word. This demonstrates how grace can keep you beyond a specific time frame and postpone your judgment in order for you to repent and renounce your crimes. You can cast out demons, tie and loose, but if you do not repent, your own judgment will be severe. Saul was given the order to smite and destroy Amalek, slaughtering men and women, children and sucklings, cow and sheep, camels and asses.

Remember that he obtained the mission to Amalek while disobeying and rebelling against God. As a result, seeing visions, prophesying, binding, and casting out demons while living in sin is not a permission to continue in your sins. You could be nearing the end of your grace period. When his spiritual throne was taken away from him, Saul gathered God's army and proceeded to Amalek.

Today, many offices and positions of leadership are vacant before God, despite the fact that they are occupied by disobedient, wicked, and rejected elders. It is only a matter of time before the selected people see David ascend to the throne. Saul was given precise instructions, yet he ignored them.

"But Saul and the people spared Agag, and the best of the sheep, and of the oxen, and of the fatlings, and the lambs, and all that was good, and would not utterly destroy them: but everything that was vile and refuse, that they destroyed utterly. Then came the word of the Lord unto Samuel, saying, it repenteth me that I have set up Saul to be king: for he is turned back from following me, and hath not performed my commandments. And it grieved Samuel; and he cried unto the Lord all night. And when Samuel rose early to meet Saul in the morning, it was told Samuel, saying, Saul came to Carmel, and, behold, he set him up a place, and is gone about, and passed on, and gone down to Gilgal" (1 Samuel 15:9-12).

There are gospel preachers, leaders, and labourers who live in sin while controlling enormous congregations of real believers. They construct large cathedrals, live in mansions, drive the greatest automobiles, have large bank accounts, and wage war against Satan and God's adversaries. These things are not inherently wrong, but the main concern is one's spiritual status before God. Do not be misled by the large crowd that is following you. While Saul remained king, the audience still followed him, but the throne had been spiritually taken away from him.

Millions of God's true children follow many corrupt ministers and general overseers. Wealthy born-again Christians fund ministries, pay tithes, make special sacrifices, and plant seeds, but they live in deception. They give good sermons and command a lot of respect, but they breach marital vows and have hidden sexual encounters. Despite the fact that King Saul had broken his connection with God, he marched into the city of Amalek and waited in the valley to fight God's battle. Saul preached to the Kenites to separate from the immoral nation of Amalek in order to prevent destruction, despite the fact that he himself has refused to separate from sin.

Going to church, praying, answering God's call, preaching, or carrying out divine assignment in part is insufficient. God expects complete commitment and obedience to His Word, call, and mission for us. God gave King Saul the task of destroying everything the Amalekites possessed and not sparing them. He was tasked with killing man and woman, new-born and suckling, ox and sheep, camel and ass, but he spared Agag. He saved the best sheep, cows, fatlings, lambs, and all the other nice animals.

"And Samuel came to Saul: and Saul said unto him, blessed be thou of the Lord: I have performed the commandment of the Lord. And Samuel said, what meaneth then this bleating of the sheep in mine ears, and the lowing of the oxen which I hear? And Saul said, they have brought them from the Amalekites: for the people spared the best of the sheep and of the oxen, to sacrifice unto the Lord thy God; and the rest we have utterly destroyed. Then Samuel said unto Saul, Stay, and I will tell thee what the Lord hath said to me this night. And he said unto him, Say on. And Samuel said, when thou wast little in thine own sight, wast thou not made the head of the tribes of Israel, and the Lord anointed thee king over Israel?" (1 Samuel 15:13-17).

We might conclude from this that ministers and believers who have the power and God's grace to overcome sin but choose to allow particular sins to reign over their life may invite the spirit of witchcraft into their lives, families, and ministries. The good news is that God's grace is always enough for us.

"For the grace of God that bringeth salvation hath appeared to all men, teaching us that, denying ungodliness and worldly lusts, we should live soberly, righteously, and godly, in this present world" (Titus 2:11-12).

"For God hath not called us unto uncleanness, but unto holiness. He therefore that despiseth, despiseth not man, but God, who hath also given unto us His Holy Spirit" (1 Thessalonians 4:7-8).

God cannot call you to any task unless He provides you with the power and grace to complete it. When God appointed Saul as King of Israel, He anointed, commissioned, and enabled him to complete his task. That is why you have the option of living in sin, in complete or partial compliance. Individual choices of all individuals, not God's will, cause us to languish in sin. You and I have the ability to oppose the devil, deny ungodliness, worldliness, and lusts, and live soberly, righteously, and godly in this present world. Saul had all the authority he needed to entirely obey God, but he chose to go the other way in order to save what God had rejected. What God deemed wicked, Saul called good, and he saved Agag, whom God had sentenced to death.

"And the Lord sent thee on a journey, and said, go and utterly destroy the sinners the Amalekites, and fight against them until they be consumed. Wherefore then didst thou not obey the voice of the Lord, but didst fly upon the spoil, and didst evil in the sight of the Lord? And Saul said unto Samuel, Yea, I have obeyed the voice of the Lord, and have gone the way which the Lord sent me, and have brought Agag the king of Amalek, and have utterly

destroyed the Amalekites. But the people took of the spoil, sheep and oxen, the chief of the things which should have been utterly destroyed, to sacrifice unto the Lord thy God in Gilgal" (1 Samuel 15:18-21).

It is incorrect to defend your justifications for continuing to sin and defy God's command. Whoever continues to sin or disobey God's command is inviting the spirit of witchcraft to rule and reign over his or her life. To remain in sin is to displease God, which is an act of witchcraft, and God may withdraw His Spirit from you after a series of warnings. When God removes His Spirit, the demonic spirit of occultism takes complete possession. When you begin to argue and act against well-established truths such as marriage doctrine, holiness, and so on, you may have been initiated into occultism without realizing it. When you sin or make mistakes and fail to admit the truth and repent, you may have unknowingly accepted occultism. Obedience to God's Word and commandments is superior to any sacrifice you can imagine.

"And Samuel said, Hath the Lord as great delight in burnt offerings and sacrifices, as in obeying the voice of the Lord? Behold, to obey is better than sacrifice, and to hearken than the fat of rams. For rebellion is as the sin of witchcraft, and stubbornness is as iniquity and idolatry. Because thou hast rejected the word of the Lord, he hath also rejected thee from being king. And Saul said unto Samuel, I have sinned: for I have transgressed the commandment of the Lord, and thy words: because I feared the people, and obeyed their voice. Now therefore, I pray thee, pardon my sin, and turn again with me, that I may worship the Lord. And Samuel said unto Saul, I will not return with thee: for thou hast rejected the word of the Lord, and the Lord hath rejected thee from being king over Israel" (1 Samuel 15:22-26).

"He, that being often reproved hardeneth his neck, shall suddenly be destroyed, and that without remedy" (Proverbs 29:1).

If you continue to argue against the truth and reject God's warnings until your period of grace expires, your judgment may be final. Sin without remorse, restitution, and abstinence from wrongdoing is an invitation to the witchcraft kingdom. Living in sin without guilt can imply entire acceptance or obedience to witchcraft, and once established, you have become an occult member by proxy. Any transgression you commit as a preacher or servant of God, knowing well that you are violating God's Word, is nothing more than approval of witchcraft and occultism.

Many senior ministers and believers do not engage in immoral behaviour, but they are hesitant to confront members who are living in sin for fear of losing them. This is complicity, which in law is considered commission. It is really odd that certain men of God interact with infamous killers and sinners. When such men inspire their associates, killers on their behalf will go out and kill innocent people. They may not use their words to request that people kill for them, but their body language does so while they pretend to be unaware of such horrible activities. That is why, when such persons make mistakes, they cannot be suspended or punished because they work for them covertly.

When you continue to allow one or more sins to reign over your life, God is not concerned in the number of people who attend your ministry or the volume of labour you accomplish. Only those in the occult who would not reprimand or remove famous sinners from their midst. God will not be pleased with your offerings and sacrifices if you continue to only partially obey Him. Rebellion and disobedience are the sins that lead to witchcraft and occultism. King Saul was obstinate and rebellious, which caused him to commit crimes and practice idolatry, which is occultism. He persisted until God rejected him, despite many warnings from God's prophet.

"And as Samuel turned about to go away, he laid hold upon the skirt of his mantle, and it rent. And Samuel said unto him, The Lord hath rent the kingdom of Israel from thee this day, and hath given it to a neighbor of thine, that

23

is better than thou. And also, the Strength of Israel will not

lie nor repent: for he is not a man, that he should repent.

Then he said, I have sinned: yet honor me now, I pray thee,

before the elders of my people, and before Israel, and turn

again with me, that I may worship the Lord thy God. So,

Samuel turned again after Saul; and Saul worshipped the

Lord" (1 Samuel 15:27-31).

It doesn't matter how many times you sin or how many times you confess your sins. What counts is how ready and determined you are to give up your sins for good. When you sin and God turns away from you, if you truly apologize and give up your sins for good, he will forgive you, no matter how bad or disgusting your sins are. It is better to admit your mistakes and leave them behind for good.

"He that covereth his sins shall not prosper: but whoso confesseth and forsaketh them shall have mercy" (Proverbs 28:13).

"Come now, and let us reason together, saith the Lord: though your sins be as scarlet, they shall be as white as snow; though they be red like crimson, they shall be as wool" (Isaiah 1:18).

"Come unto me, all ye that labor and are heavy laden, and I will give you rest" (Matthew 11:28).

God can forgive every wrongdoing.. However, forgiveness must be really sought after. If you are sincerely ready and willing to repent of your sins, God will forgive you. Your sins may be as scarlet as blood, but if you are willing and determined to repent, they will be as white as snow and wool. God could not have asked people to seek forgiveness if He was unwilling to pardon their misdeeds. 'Come all ye that labour and are heavy laden, and I will give you rest,' Jesus answered, 'I am the way, the truth, and the life.'

The thief at Christ's right hand on the cross repented, and despite all his sins, horrors, slaughter, and awful acts, Christ forgave him, cleansed him, and immediately took him to Paradise. Saul's situation was much different. His repentance was not accompanied by a conscious decision to abandon his misdeeds and practices.

"But I say unto you, that it shall be more tolerable for the land of Sodom in the day of judgment, than for thee. At that time Jesus answered and said, I thank thee, O Father, Lord of heaven and earth, because thou hast hid these things from the wise and prudent, and hast revealed them unto babes" (Matthew 11:24-25).

"Then he said, I have sinned: yet honor me now, I pray thee, before the elders of my people, and before Israel, and turn again with me, that I may worship the Lord thy God. So, Samuel turned again after Saul; and Saul worshipped the Lord" (1 Samuel 15:30-31).

Have you ever thought about why God didn't forgive King Saul after he admitted and confessed his sins? (See 1 Samuel 15:24-31). The reason is simple: He didn't want to give up his sins, and his worship was fake, imperfect, and shallow. God knows everything that's in your heart. So He knows if you're ready or not to stop doing the bad things you've admitted to. These are sins that Saul admitted to and never gave up:

- He made a sacrifice he didn't have the right to make.
- He saved King Agag, whom God had told to die.
- He was mad that David was more popular than him.
- He did everything he could to kill David. (1 Samuel 13:8-14; 14:37; 15:8-15, 22-23; 18:8-11).
- He chose and made plans to give David to the Philistines so they could kill him.
- David was tricked and couldn't enjoy his marriage to his daughter.
- His first son Jonathan told him the truth, so he cursed him.

- He killed the priest Ahimelech and his family because they were friends with David. (1 Samuel 18:17, 19, 25, 28; 19:1-7, 10-11, 14-15, 19-24; 20:27, 31-34; 21:7; 22:9-23).
- King Saul asked a woman whose spirit he knew for help. (1 Samuel 28:7-25; 31:1-13).

You become an occultist by worshiping an idol, joining an evil group, continuing in the occult group, and engaging in wickedness. By refusing to repent and abandon your connection, you can inherit witchcraft from your occult parents and prosper in witchcraft or occultism. These are true events. And so are the curses they receive. For example, Jeremiah was cautioned as follows:

"The word of the Lord came also unto me, saying, thou shalt not take thee a wife, neither shalt thou have sons or daughters in this place. For thus saith the Lord concerning the sons and concerning the daughters that are born in this

place, and concerning their mothers that bare them, and concerning their fathers that begat them in this land; They shall die of grievous deaths; they shall not be lamented; neither shall they be buried; but they shall be as dung upon the face of the earth: and they shall be consumed by the sword, and by famine; and their carcasses shall be meat for the fowls of heaven, and for the beasts of the earth"

(Jeremiah 16:1-4).

By continuing to disobey God's Word, you remain a witch, wizard, and occult person. Consulting familiar spirits or being idolatrous strengthens your occult membership. When you marry a witch or wizard and reject God's Word, you open yourself up to the attack of witchcraft powers. Some folks gripe and wonder why my troubles haven't gone away despite my prayers, fasting, and deliverances. Why am I experiencing roadblocks at the brink of breakthroughs? Why do I have recurring issues, continual defeats and failures, and why am I always attacked?

Many people are perplexed because, no matter how hard they strive, they are rejected and despised. They are constantly hounded and pursued in their dreams, and they are literally denied their rights, perks, and entitlements. They are plagued by unusual illnesses, persecution, and anguish, and they lack true aid. Some people dream of their birthplaces, old school uniforms, even exams they took many years ago and passed physically. Many others have sex and do all kinds of strange things in their dreams?

Many victims of witchcraft suffer inconceivable failures, poverty, marital problems, and the inability to maintain healthy connections. They constantly seem to run into the wrong folks wherever they go. Some people endure defeats, failures, marital problems, divorce, miscarriages, painful menstruations, thwarted delight, and happiness. Many people struggle for a long time before they achieve anything substantial. While many people make poor decisions and suffer as a result, others are constantly misunderstood, misrepresented, abandoned by actual helpers, and suffer alone without assistance.

Witchcraft victims suffer from a severe loss of pleasant things, debts, lack in the midst of plenty, shame, censure, and dishonour. Many people who have been estranged from God due to perplexing circumstances turn for aid in the wrong places. They are oppressed, confined, limited, frail, and ill. They have commercial failures, endless struggles, work where others harvest, and wish to die out of frustration. If you are going through any of these experiences and have questions, here are some answers that may help you -

"And it shall come to pass, when thou shalt shew this people all these words, and they shall say unto thee, Wherefore hath the LORD pronounced all this great evil against us? Or what is our iniquity? Or what is our sin that we have committed against the LORD our God? Then shalt thou say unto them, Because your fathers have forsaken me, saith the LORD, and have walked after other gods, and have served them, and have worshipped them, and have forsaken me, and have not kept my law; And ye have

done worse than your fathers; for, behold, ye walk every
one after the imagination of his evil heart, that they may
not hearken unto me" (Jeremiah 16:10-12).

Sin divides us from God, true joy, riches, serenity, and all that is good in this world. It is not enough to say you are a Christian, a minister, or a worker in God's house. It is not sufficient to state that you have been a born-again Christian for many years or that you were born into a Christian family. God expects fruits of repentance regardless of your Christian status or age. Repentance, confession, restitution, and forsaking of sins committed or inherited are required.

You must learn more about your foundation and the faults that plague your root. You must avoid any harmful parental traditions. You cannot live in sin, profess to be born-again, and complain about your circumstances. True, a Christian can be assaulted and oppressed, but we must not suffer as unbelievers and sinners do since our burden in Christ is light.

"Take my yoke upon you, and learn of me; for I am meek and lowly in heart: and ye shall find rest unto your souls. For my yoke is easy, and my burden is light" (Matthew 11:29-30).

If you accept Jesus as your personal Lord and Saviour, your yoke can be broken and all your pain can end. In its place, you will have divine joy and peace. Because of this, Paul the Apostle told us to always be strong in the Lord and in His power.

"Finally, my brethren, be strong in the Lord, and in the power of his might. Put on the whole armor of God, that ye may be able to stand against the wiles of the devil. For we wrestle not against flesh and blood, but against principalities, against powers, against the rulers of the darkness of this world, against spiritual wickedness in high places" (Ephesians 6:10-12).

You can be entirely delivered if you have an inherited witchcraft spirit and surrender to Christ. What if you were drawn to occultism on purpose or inherited it? You can also be delivered and entirely set free. All you have to do is be strong, have faith in God and His capacity to deliver, and then pray. Put on all of God's gear and stand firm against sin, Satan, and bad traditions. Refuse to return to sin. Put on righteousness as a garment, have faith in God, and earnestly defend your salvation. Allow your relationship with God to be strong, and always pray until something new occurs.

"My little children, these things write I unto you, that ye sin not. And if any man sin, we have an advocate with the Father, Jesus Christ the righteous" (1 John 2:1).

"He that covereth his sins shall not prosper: but whoso confesseth and forsaketh them shall have mercy" (Proverbs 28:13).

If you sin by accident or for any other cause, do not hesitate in repenting. Delaying allows the devil to blame you before God. Repent and abandon your misdeeds right away. It is preferable to first report yourself to Christ, our advocate with the Father, so that by the time the devil accuses you before God, Christ must have spoken to the Father on your behalf. As King Saul did, you must bear the fruits of the Spirit and conquer pride and pointless arguments. Be as quick as the devil, as David.

"Have mercy upon me, O God, according to thy lovingkindness: according unto the multitude of thy tender mercies blot out my transgressions. Wash me thoroughly from mine iniquity, and cleanse me from my sin. For I acknowledge my transgressions: and my sin is ever before me. Against thee, thee only, have I sinned, and done this evil in thy sight: that thou mightiest be justified when thou speakest, and be clear when thou judgest" (Psalms 51:1-4).

It is preferable to repent as soon as possible. Request God's mercy, the display of His loving-kindness, and the erasure of your trespasses. Repent completely and completely, and ask God to wash you of your sins through the blood of Jesus. Recognize your mistakes. When you know you are guilty, do not disguise it, transfer blame, or pretend innocence.

"But the fruit of the Spirit is love, joy, peace, longsuffering, gentleness, goodness, faith, Meekness, temperance: against such there is no law" (Galatians 5:22-23).

When you live by the fruit of the Spirit, God's grace protects you from pride, envy, and other vices. You will treasure your joy and tranquillity in God and will never abandon your faith. You would rather suffer and die than lose your connection with God. A man or woman after God's own heart will always obey God and keep His commands. Such people are usually gentle in nature and are never in a hurry to accomplish unproductive goals if eternity is on their minds. You must always do the right thing and be kind to others. You must faithfully protect your beliefs even if it means death.

God's Spirit will assist you in being meek and having a nice disposition in order to satisfy God and wait for His deliverance. If you bear the fruits of the Spirit, you will be delivered eventually, no matter how long you suffer.

"Shall the prey be taken from the mighty, or the lawful captive delivered? But thus, saith the Lord, Even the captives of the mighty shall be taken away, and the prey of the terrible shall be delivered: for I will contend with him that contendeth with thee, and I will save thy children. And I will feed them that oppress thee with their own flesh; and they shall be drunken with their own blood, as with sweet wine: and all flesh shall know that I the Lord am thy Savior and thy Redeemer, the mighty One of Jacob" (Isaiah 49:24-26).

Your adversary or difficulty may have driven you away from everything wonderful in life, yet they cannot permanently separate you from God's divine assistance, deliverance, and blessings. The devil can use all of his powers against you, but God's deliverance can save you. All the wicked powers of the occult and the powers of your father's house pale in comparison to God's deliverance power. Your destiny may have been taken by all the altars on earth, in the rivers, and in the heavens, yet God is able to deliver you now.

Witchcraft animals and fish in the seas may have gobbled up your destiny, but they will all regurgitate you at the appointed moment. Allow them to devour your marriage, destiny, reproductive organs, finances, or health if they so desire, but when God appears, you will be fully delivered. If you are a Christian and have lost everything of life's good things as a result, you will undoubtedly recover everything, just as Job and David did. God will finally end every wicked assignment in your life, no matter how awful your case is right now or how strong your opponents are.

If you sincerely repent, confess your sins, and resolve to forsake them, God will enter the battlefield of your life and begin to fight your adversaries. Your prayers and decrees may not only deliver you or save your children, but they may also keep you safe from your adversaries. God has the power to feed your foes and oppressors with their own flesh till they perish. God wants to demonstrate to your enemies and issues that He is in charge of your life, not them. He, not they, is the LORD. He, not them, is your Saviour. God is your sole saviour; he is the Mighty One of Israel and the Creator of Heaven and Earth.

Every earthly difficulty goes through the gates of hell, and Christ said that the gates of hell would not prevail against you and me. Do you realize that if you sincerely repent and forsake all your sins, you are entitled to the keys to God's kingdom? Do you realize that you can bind anything on Earth, including all of your problems, with these keys? Do you realize that even if you lose your health, marriage, or finances here on Earth, the gods will support you? Do you also know that whatever you bind here on earth, heaven will not challenge you, let alone the devil, witches, wizards, and occult people on earth? Do you realize it also applies to the things you can lose on Earth? Do you know that if you combine your faith with mine in a prayer of agreement, we can have whatever we want? Do you realize that God, our Father, can hear agreement or decree prayers from each believer or the entire church in heaven?

"And I say also unto thee, that thou art Peter, and upon this rock I will build my church; and the gates of hell shall not prevail against it. And I will give unto thee the keys of the kingdom of heaven: and whatsoever thou shalt bind on earth shall be bound in heaven: and whatsoever thou shalt loose on earth shall be loosed in heaven" (Matthew 16:18-19).

Do you realize that impossible things do not exist in the presence of believers who can pray, decree, and believe God? Do you know that simply trusting any word you hear right now might start your deliverance process? Because of this, Noah did not perish in his generation, and God accepted his contribution. Abraham heard and believed the word in his old age, and God blessed him with a kid, Isaac. God altered Jacob's name to become a blessing to nations when he heard and believed God's promises. That is what Moses' parents heard and believed, and they refused to hand over Moses to be slain. Moses regularly received the Word of Promise from his parents, and he abandoned Egypt's throne to become a national deliverance minister unlike any other. That is what prompted Moses to request that Pharaoh release the children of Israel to serve the one and only true God. Today, listen to this:

"Whatsoever ye shall bind on earth shall be bound in heaven: and whatsoever ye shall loose on earth shall be loosed in heaven. Again, I say unto you, that if two of you shall agree on earth as touching anything that they shall ask, it shall be done for them of my Father which is in

heaven. For where two or three are gathered together in my name, there am I in the midst of them" (Matthew 18:18-20).

The Word of God is swift, strong, and sharper than any two-edged sword, penetrating even to the dividing asunder of soul and spirit, joints and marrow, and a discerner of the thoughts and intentions of the heart (Hebrews_4:12). Because there were no blood covers, Egyptian families lost their firstborn children due to a lack of confidence in the Word. Faith in the Word freed an entire captive nation from Egypt. Faith in the Word split the Red Sea, allowing a redeemed people to pass across. What would you do if you suddenly realized that the entire creature is expecting you to appear?

"For the earnest expectation of the creature waiteth for the manifestation of the sons of God" (Romans 8:19).

The entire creation is waiting for your command on what to do, and they will obey you. When the sun heard Joshua's command, it obeyed. The moon remained motionless until Joshua had completely defeated his adversaries. When Samson said a word of faith, the building collapsed, killing the Philistines. Hannah ventured out in faith, and her barrenness allowed Samuel to emerge as a famous prophet in Israel. Elijah spoke the word, and the heavens stopped raining for three years. The heavens opened as he decreed again.

Elisha said the word, and the woman of Shunammite's locked womb opened, and she bore a son. The same word brought back the dead. When Hezekiah issued the command, angels descended from heaven and slaughtered 185,000 warriors in his adversary's camp. He spoke again, and death avoided him for the next fifteen years. Poverty, pain, and want vanished from Jabez's life when he pronounced the word through faith, and his coast was enlarged with genuine blessings overflowing in his house.

What else is there to say? What about Daniel and his three Hebrew buddies, who found favour in a foreign place and were able to prosper and fulfil their destiny? What about Esther, her uncle Mordechai, Nehemiah, Ezra, and the others who refused to accept defeat and instead prayed until something happened? Christ healed all kind of ailments and diseases in the middle of witchcraft crusades and demonic revivals. He cured lepers, healed those with palsy, delivered the downtrodden, dealt with graveyard demons, opened blind eyes, fed the poor, and collected taxes for his believers.

God's Word is still available to you and me today. When Jesus restored withered hands, dealt with plagues, calmed storms, healed woman with issue of blood, prospered people who toiled all night, and raised Lazarus from the dead after four days in the grave, He said the same Word. The same Word you are hearing now was taught by Christ's followers, and five thousand sinners repented. They annihilated many illnesses and diseases, and sorcerers who refused to repent were blinded. A repentant

Paul was cured and liberated from the sentence of blindness by the same Word, and he was given the authority to demolish Gentile gods. What are you waiting for now? How much longer would you wait before speaking God's Word?

CHAPTER THREE

Freedom from Occultism

J onathan, Saul's first son, made the decision to fear God
and preserve truth at the cost of his life, while Saul's
other sons and close allies were forced into initiation into
occultism and witchcraft. Jonathan didn't care who God
put on the throne, all he cared about was that the children
of Israel were delivered and triumphed. That's not very
important to him (cf. 1 Samuel 14:1-32). This is why, with
the exception of Jonathan, Saul's other slaves followed his
orders to assassinate David without provocation.

"And Saul spake to Jonathan his son, and to all his
servants, that they should kill David. But Jonathan Saul's
son delighted much in David: and Jonathan told David,
saying, Saul my father seeketh to kill thee: now therefore, I
pray thee, take heed to thyself until the morning, and abide
in a secret place, and hide thyself: And I will go out and
stand beside my father in the field where thou art, and I

*will commune with my father of thee; and what I see, that
I will tell thee" (1 Samuel 19:1-3).*

Jonathan told David the secret before he would
respectfully share it with his father in private. Jonathan
was preaching righteousness to his father as the plot to
assassinate David was being hatched around him. At first,
he defended David to his father, painting him in a positive
light and reminding him of how much he had cared for
and admired David.

*"And Jonathan spake good of David unto Saul his father,
and said unto him, Let not the king sin against his servant,
against David; because he hath not sinned against thee,
and because his works have been to thee-ward very good:
For he did put his life in his hand, and slew the Philistine,
and the Lord wrought a great salvation for all Israel: thou
sawest it, and didst rejoice: wherefore then wilt thou sin
against innocent blood, to slay David without a cause?*

47

And Saul hearkened unto the voice of Jonathan: and Saul sw: As the Lord liveth, he shall not be slain. And Jonathan called David, and Jonathan shewed him all those things. And Jonathan brought David to Saul, and he was in his presence, as in times past" (1 Samuel 19:4-7).

Jonathan wisely reminded his father how David risked his life to defeat Goliath, the Philistine, and how God used him to bring redemption to all Israel. He made his father, Saul, remember how happy he was when he saw what God used David to do to Israel's foes. He also warned his father that slaying David was tantamount to attacking God by bleeding unjustified innocent blood. Despite Jonathan's advice and admonitions, Saul was determined to kill David. When the evil spirit of murder overtook Saul, he attempted to kill David personally or used anybody around him to do it, save Jonathan.

"And the evil spirit from the Lord was upon Saul, as he sat in his house with his javelin in his hand: and David played with his hand" (1 Samuel 19:9).

"Saul also sent messengers unto David's house, to watch him, and to slay him in the morning: and Michal David's wife told him, saying, if thou save not thy life to night, tomorrow thou shalt be slain" (1 Samuel 19:11).

The lesson here is that if you let any boss, witch, or wizard use you to do bad things, you are in the power of witchcraft and occultism's bondage. Jonathan made it clear where he stood and spoke out against evil, witches, and occultism in his father's government. Prince Jonathan, Saul's oldest son, broke away from his family's evil pact of witchcraft and occultism by what he did. While other people in his father's family were taken as slaves, Jonathan kept himself, his children, and their children's children from being forced to do bad things. David liked him so much that he loved him like a brother.

"Therefore, thou shalt deal kindly with thy servant; for thou hast brought thy servant into a covenant of the Lord with thee: notwithstanding, if there be in me iniquity, slay me thyself; for why shouldest thou bring me to thy father?"

(1 Samuel 20:8).

"And thou shalt not only while yet I live shew me the kindness of the Lord, that I die not" (1 Samuel 20:14).

"And Saul said unto his servants, provide me now a man that can play well, and bring him to me" (1 Samuel 16:17).

Jonathan had the choice to remain a prince with all the perks that come with being a crowned prince, but he decided to enter into a holy covenant with a fugitive in order to remain in God's good book. He made a holy covenant with David on behalf of himself, his children, born and unborn, for all time. Saul was enraged by his acts and determination to preserve David from his father, and he cursed Jonathan, his first son. It is preferable to be cursed by a man rather than by God.

"Then Saul's anger was kindled against Jonathan, and he said unto him, thou son of the perverse rebellious woman, do not I know that thou hast chosen the son of Jesse to thine own confusion, and unto the confusion of thy mother's nakedness? For as long as the son of Jesse liveth upon the ground, thou shalt not be established, nor thy kingdom. Wherefore now send and fetch him unto me, for he shall surely die. And Jonathan answered Saul his father, and said unto him, wherefore shall he be slain? What hath he done? And Saul cast a javelin at him to smite him: whereby Jonathan knew that it was determined of his father to slay David" (1 Samuel 20:30-33).

To spare David's life, Jonathan advised him to avoid the national feast and open gatherings until he received security clearance. When Saul discovered that Jonathan had tipped David off, he cursed him, stating, 'As long as David was alive, he and his kingdom (meaning Jonathan's kingdom) shall not be established.' When King Saul announced that David must die, everyone agreed except Jonathan, who questioned his father about the justification for David's death. At that point, King Saul threw a javelin at him in an attempt to slay him, but Jonathan nevertheless imparted the secret to David. Jonathan's father must have denied him his rights, benefits, and entitlements as a result of his son's fight for justice. But, at the perfect time, David recalled Jonathan's love and loyalty to him.

"And David said, is there yet any that is left of the house of Saul, that I may shew him kindness for Jonathan's sake? And there was of the house of Saul a servant whose name was Ziba. And when they had called him unto David, the

king said unto him, Art thou Ziba? And he said, thy

servant is he" (2 Samuel 9:1-2).

When Jonathan died, David sobbed deeply and fasted till sunset since his greatest buddy had been killed by the enemy's sword. 'My brother Jonathan, very pleasant hast thou been unto me,' David said of Jonathan. I am concerned for thee, thy love to me was magnificently, surpassing the love of women,' and he commanded the females of Israel to mourn for Jonathan's death. When the time came, David attempted to reciprocate Jonathan's kindness –

"And David said, is there yet any that is left of the house of Saul, that I may shew him kindness for Jonathan's sake?"

(2 Samuel 9:1).

"And the king said, is there not yet any of the house of Saul, that I may shew the kindness of God unto him? And

Ziba said unto the king, Jonathan hath yet a son, which is lame on his feet" (2 Samuel 9:3).

"Then the king called to Ziba, Saul's servant, and said unto him, I have given unto thy master's son all that pertained to Saul and to all his house" (2 Samuel 9:9).

Even though Jonathan died before David, the promise they made to each other was never broken, and their acts of kindness kept going even after they were gone. When King Saul used witchcraft and occultism, he had the support of the whole country and was in charge of its money. Everyone on his side was very rich, powerful, and successful. Except for Jonathan, all of his children were at the top of their lives and had everything good they could want. They had all the money and must have thought Jonathan was a fool because he wouldn't join in with occultism and witches.

In reality, combining witchcraft and occultism in order to get ahead and live well is foolish and narrow-minded. It is a bad deal because you are selling your birthright, ruining your future and forever, and hurting your children who are already born and those who are yet to be born. It is better to have to suffer because of a holy agreement than to have to suffer forever because of occultism and witchcraft. When David's replies started to show up, King Saul's empire of witchcraft had already fallen apart, and he had lost everything, including his family. Everyone in Saul's family who was sensible was either dead, sick, poor, or had very little of anything good. When the evil forces of destruction were done with Saul, they attacked Jonathan's son Mephibosheth with lame and crippled him. This was probably because Saul didn't pray. At that time, he didn't have a home of his own because his grandpa, Saul, had lost all the money he once had.

"And the king said unto him, where is he? And Ziba said unto the king, Behold, he is in the house of Machir, the son

of Ammiel, in Lodebar. Then king David sent, and fetched him out of the house of Machir, the son of Ammiel, from Lodebar. Now when Mephibosheth, the son of Jonathan, the son of Saul, was come unto David, he fell on his face, and did reverence. And David said, Mephibosheth. And he answered, Behold thy servant! And David said unto him, Fear not: for I will surely shew thee kindness for Jonathan thy father's sake, and will restore thee all the land of Saul thy father; and thou shalt eat bread at my table continually. And he bowed himself, and said, what is thy servant, that thou shouldest look upon such a dead dog as I am?" (2 Samuel 9:4-8).

Even though he was lame, David was very kind to him because his father had made a promise to David. David also gave him back everything that his grandpa Saul had lost because of witchcraft and occultism. Even though he was a prince, he was very poor because his grandpa was evil and used witchcraft and occultism. So, why did Mephibosheth have to go through all of these bad things?

He became lame, poor, a servant, and was as good as dead. It was probably because he didn't know what his rights, benefits, and entitlements were and didn't want to fight for them through prayers and spiritual battle.

"And afterward when David heard it, he said, I and my kingdom are guiltless before the Lord forever from the blood of Abner the son of Ner: Let it rest on the head of Joab, and on all his father's house; and let there not fail from the house of Joab one that hath an issue, or that is a leper, or that leaneth on a staff, or that falleth on the sword, or that lacketh bread" (2 Samuel 3:28-29).

If you do not fight for your rights as a believer, your inheritance and home may be taken over by strangers. Reproach, shame, and disgrace may be your lot in life. A prince who does not fight his battles may become a servant to his servant or die before his time, leaving his children fatherless and his wife widowed (see Lamentation 5:1-22).

This could apply to Christians as well. When David returned from exile following Saul's death, he learned that the witchcraft, wicked things, and sacrifices Saul performed with his occult circle had blocked the skies.

"Then there was a famine in the days of David three years, year after year; and David enquired of the Lord. And the Lord answered, it is for Saul, and for his bloody house, because he slew the Gibeonites" (2 Samuel 21:1).

Occultists, witches, and wizards took over all of Israel's good things, including cash and positions. Famine, dearth, sickness, sicknesses, reproaches, and dishonour afflicted the entire nation of Israel. David and his prayer team began to pray, reminding God that the earth and all its fullness; the world and all who dwell in it belongs to Him. They prayed for divine prosperity, knowing full well that the righteous are the legitimate owners and heir apparent of the creatures.

"This is the generation of them that seek him, that seek thy face, O Jacob. Selah. Lift up your heads, O ye gates; and be ye lift up, ye everlasting doors; and the King of glory shall come in" (Psalms 24:6-7).

God commanded that the heads of witches, wizards, and occult organisations who erected hurdles to believers' actual prosperity be lifted. At the same time, all the demons summoned by evil sacrifices were killed, and everlasting portals opened for the King of Glory to reclaim the nation for believers. Curses against believers were lifted, and prosperity was restored. Witches', magicians', and sinners' enterprises began to fail.

When believers pray for divine visitation, God appears with a two-edged sword, separating some individuals to be blessed and others to be cursed, bringing judgment to some and freedom to others. Only eight men remained alive when King Saul's family was visited for judgment. Only eight men survived from a family that once had many able men and young bright young men under national security direction. Following that, seven people were captured and handed over to their ruthless foes to be slaughtered.

"And the Gibeonites said unto him, we will have no silver nor gold of Saul, nor of his house; neither for us shalt thou kill any man in Israel. And he said, what ye shall say, that will I do for you. And they answered the king, the man that consumed us, and that devised against us that we should be destroyed from remaining in any of the coasts of Israel, let seven men of his sons be delivered unto us, and we will hang them up unto the Lord in Gibeah of Saul, whom the Lord did choose. And the king said, I will give them" (2 Samuel 21:4-6).

If you are cursed by witchcraft or occultism, the spirit of pain, hardship, sickness, and death will always find you and destroy you, no matter where you hide. Problems that others easily overcome will cling to you and not leave until you are consumed, unless you sincerely repent and quit your misdeeds. Unrepentant sinners face problems that push them to spend all of their money, defy all remedies, and take away everything nice before killing them when they needed their life the most. The sons of Gibeonites told David that they desired neither silver, gold, or the lives of anybody else in Israel except the seven men from Saul's house. The judgment of unrepentant witchcraft or occultism practitioners is merciless. They expire gradually in painful deaths during their judgment.

"The word of the Lord came also unto me, saying, thou shalt not take thee a wife, neither shalt thou have sons or daughters in this place. For thus saith the Lord concerning the sons and concerning the daughters that are born in this place, and concerning their mothers that bare them, and concerning their fathers that begat them in this land; They shall die of grievous deaths; they shall not be lamented; neither shall they be buried; but they shall be as dung upon the face of the earth: and they shall be consumed by the

sword, and by famine; and their carcasses shall be meat for

the fowls of heaven, and for the beasts of the earth"

(Jeremiah 16:1-4).

On their judgment days, the majority of them lose the things that bring them the most joy. Some people are absorbed by their health, marriages, peace, joy, happiness, helpers, body organs, or finances before they die. Others may see it as their enterprises, occupations, abilities, or anything else intended to make them known on the planet. Anyone who attempts to assist them is attacked and frustrated until they abandon their good intentions or perish trying. People everywhere despise, reject, and fight them for no apparent reason. Such people, and many others around them, were continually perplexed as to 'WHY?'

"And it shall come to pass, when thou shalt shew this

people all these words, and they shall say unto thee,

wherefore hath the Lord pronounced all this great evil against us? or what is our iniquity? or what is our sin that we have committed against the Lord our God? Then shalt thou say unto them, Because your fathers have forsaken me, saith the Lord, and have walked after other gods, and have served them, and have worshipped them, and have forsaken me, and have not kept my law; And ye have done worse than your fathers; for, behold, ye walk everyone after the imagination of his evil heart, that they may not hearken unto me" (Jeremiah 16:10-12).

If your parents have previously served idols, conducted witchcrafts, divination, and enchantment, or belonged to occult societies or the witchcraft kingdom, you require deliverance. Your confession as a born-again Christian, as well as your deliverance from sin, do not exempt or excuse you from working out your own salvation with fear and trembling. They ensure that you have enough strength to fight for your rights by remaining in Christ and engaging in spiritual warfare. Ignorance about a believer's dominion in the spiritual sphere might lead to such a believer becoming unconcerned about never-ending spiritual warfare until grave loss occurs. Our only hope for victory is to put on the whole armor of God; else, you may become a victim like the seven sons of Saul during the time of visitation.

"But the king took the two sons of Rizpah the daughter of Aiah, whom she bare unto Saul, Armoni and Mephibosheth; and the five sons of Michal the daughter of Saul, whom she brought up for Adriel the son of Barzillai the Meholathite: And he delivered them into the hands of the Gibeonites, and they hanged them in the hill before the Lord: and they fell all seven together, and were put to death in the days of harvest, in the first days, in the beginning of barley harvest" (2 Samuel 21:8-9).

The seven Saul family members were handed into the hands of their enemies. Many people nowadays are suffering from terrible pains and other issues as a result of being handed into the clutches of their spiritual foes. If you are a sincere believer and your marriage, health, joy, business, or wealth are under jeopardy, you can release them today by the grace of God.

The remaining seven young men in King Saul's household were delivered over to their adversaries, but they never protested, pleaded, or petitioned God on their behalf. Even during harvest, they accepted their fate and succumbed to their opponents' wishes. They were executed on the first day of harvest, at the commencement of the barley harvest, at the last minute, just as they were going to celebrate and be celebrated.

To avoid judgment from basic bondage, witches, or relentless adversaries from the occult realm, you must always be strong in the Lord. As a believer, spiritual lethargy is worse than unbelief.

"But the king spared Mephibosheth, the son of Jonathan

the son of Saul, because of the Lord's oath that was

between them, between David and Jonathan the son of

Saul" (2 Samuel 21:7).

"Shall the prey be taken from the mighty, or the lawful

captive delivered? But thus, saith the Lord, even the

captives of the mighty shall be taken away, and the prey of

the terrible shall be delivered: for I will contend with him

that contendeth with thee, and I will save thy children.

And I will feed them that oppress thee with their own flesh;

and they shall be drunken with their own blood, as with

sweet wine: and all flesh shall know that I the Lord am thy

Savior and thy Redeemer, the mighty One of Jacob" (Isaiah

49:24-26).

"Finally, my brethren, be strong in the Lord, and in the

power of his might" (Ephesians 6:10).

Mephibosheth was saved by his father's wisdom in standing up to his father's witchcraft and occult attacks (see 1 Samuel 19:1-7; 2 Samuel 9:1-13; 20:1-42). If you are experiencing witchcraft attacks, occult manipulation, or any other type of trouble as a believer, you must engage in spiritual battle. If you are a sinner, you must repent, confess your faults, and renounce them before praying against witchcraft and occult organisations. Even as a believer, let alone a fresh convert, you must be strong and put on all of God's armor (see Ephesians 6:10-18). In the great name of Jesus, God will undoubtedly see you through to victory.

THE SECTION OF WARFARE

DECLARATIONS TO DESTROY

INHERITED OCCULTISM

I n the name of Jesus, Almighty God, open my eyes to identify the cause of my troubles, satanic attacks, and expose them for destruction. Let the hidden mysteries of my adversaries' origins be uncovered and destroyed forever. In the name of Jesus, speak me out of the occultism and witchcraft that I wrongfully inherited. In the name of Jesus, please put an end to my hereditary witchcraft and occultism.

In the name of Jesus, I command that every act of wickedness perpetrated against me from my past be defeated by the Word of God. Any strange illness, poverty, failure, or defeat in my life since birth, your time has come to an end, and I reject you. In the name of Jesus, I release myself from idolatry and witchcraft involvement of my ancestors, parents, and relatives. In the name of Jesus, I break away from any bad influence in my life that is created by supernatural or supernormal powers to waste my life and efforts.

May Jesus' blood silence any wicked sacrifice made by my ancestors or parents that is currently harming my life and speaking against me. In the name of Jesus, I command every inherited demon, divination, charm, enchantment, or necromancer working against my destiny to perish. Any demonic being ruining my life's efforts, your time has come; I tie and cast you out. In the name of Jesus, Father Lord, rescue me from every hereditary witchcraft power, occultism, and its repercussions.

In the name of Jesus, I break free from the communal captivity of my birthplace. In the name of Jesus, anointing to fight foundational evil characters and live holy, fall upon me and deliver me from evil inheritance. Even after your deliverance, go ahead and repeat the following commands as many times as you can (Matthew 12:43-45).

OCCULTIC INVOLVEMENT

DELIVERANCE

In the name of Jesus, Father Lord, save me from first and second hand occultism and witchcraft. Please bestow upon me the ability to resist wicked characteristics. In the name of Jesus, I extinguish any occult power, sickness, disease, calamity, or evil program against me.

"And Jonathan spake good of David unto Saul his father, and said unto him, Let not the king sin against his servant, against David; because he hath not sinned against thee, and because his works have been to thee-ward very good: For he did put his life in his hand, and slew the Philistine, and the Lord wrought a great salvation for all Israel: thou sawest it, and didst rejoice: wherefore then wilt thou sin against innocent blood, to slay David without a cause? And Saul hearkened unto the voice of Jonathan: and Saul sware, As the Lord liveth, he shall not be slain. And Jonathan called David, and Jonathan shewed him all those

things. And Jonathan brought David to Saul, and he was in his presence, as in times past" (1 Samuel 19:4-7).

Wisdom from on high to avoid occultism and witchcraft attacks, possess me by force, in the name of Jesus. Any wicked personality who is trading and profiting off my destiny, your time is over; please release me immediately. In the name of Jesus, deliver me wherever they call my name for evil today. Any witchcraft fantasy created to waste my life, your time has come to an end. In the name of Jesus, I command any witchcraft coven that has arrested my destiny to catch fire and burn to ashes.

In the name of Jesus, let the altars of occultism that are working against my life be dismantled. In the name of Jesus, I command you to eliminate any witch or wizard who has promised to destroy me. Any trace of witchcraft in my life, be removed by Jesus' blood right now. In the name of Jesus, please put an end to witchcraft and occultism in my dreams. In the name of Jesus, I command that every property of witchcraft and occultism in my life catch fire and burn to ashes.

In the name of Jesus, any witch or wizard who is sitting on my destiny, blessings, and handwork, be forced to go. In the name of Jesus, Almighty God, rescue me from evil covenants and curses of occult foundation. In the name of Jesus, I command witchcraft food, water, and investment in my life to vanish.

Any odd fire that is blazing in my life from witchcraft altars, quench with Jesus' blood, in Jesus' name. In the name of Jesus, I command that any witchcraft campaign or revival taking place in my life, family, or workplace be put to an end. In the name of Jesus, I recover every good thing I have lost to witches, wizards, and occultic groups. In the name of Jesus, I withdraw from all wicked groups, known and unknown, for all time and all eternity. (Repeat this command as many times as you can, every day, week, month, and year).

3 DAYS DECLARATIONS FOR AGAINST WITCHCRAFTS ATTACKS

DAY 1

In the name of Jesus, I command that every evil plantation in my life, from whatever occultic empire, catch fire and burn to ashes. Every tribe, community, or environmental occultism in my life is ordered to catch fire and burn to ashes. In the name of Jesus, Almighty God, deliver me from inherited familial occultism. Receive deliverance immediately for everything excellent in my life that has been under occultic attack.

And he had a choice and handsome son whose name was Saul. There was not a more handsome person than he among the children of Israel. From his shoulders upward he was taller than any of the people.

Then Saul said to his servant, "Well said; come, let us go."

So they went to the city where the man of God was.

(1 Samuel 9:2, 10)

In the name of Jesus, Almighty God, restore in me the spirit of humility and renew in me your pure Spirit. Please anoint me to remember my lowly beginnings. Every occultic witchcraft voice crying out against me, be silenced by the blood of Jesus. I break free from any plan of witchcraft forces. In the name of Jesus, Almighty God, deliver me from all organized darkness and assist me to live above every evil. Every satanic program working against my destiny must be stopped. Take my destiny away from every occultic altar, Ancient of Days.

Then God blessed them, and God said to them, "Be fruitful and multiply; fill the earth and subdue it; have dominion over the fish of the sea, over the birds of the air, and over every living thing that moves on the earth." (Genesis 1:28)

In the name of Jesus, Heavenly Father, rescue me from servitude and empower me to live above every occultic force. Every occultic altar that is controlling my life must be destroyed by the Holy Spirit's fire. In the name of Jesus, I restore to you twofold what the evil empire has stolen from my life. In the name of Jesus, anoint me to be prolific, to increase and multiply; to replenish and rule other creatures. In the powerful name of Jesus, eliminate any evil entity fighting against me. Every impossibility in my life that came from the occultic kingdom, you are finished, be annihilated, in Jesus' name. I eradicate every satanic deposit in my life with the power of God Almighty. I command every organ in my body to abort every evil plantation in my body.

For this reason the king was angry and very furious, and gave the command to destroy all the wise men of Babylon.

So the decree went out, and they began killing the wise men; and they sought Daniel and his companions, to kill them. (Daniel 2:12-13)

In the name of Jesus, reveal and humiliate every satanic secret and effort to damage my life. In the name of Jesus, I return every arrow of shame, disgrace, and reproach that has been fired into my life. Blood of Jesus, free me from every evil hold. In the name of Jesus, I command every challenge in my life to propel me to the next level.

DAY 2

In the name of Jesus, I command that my name and all information about me be erased from all occultic registers. Break every shackle of occultism in my life, in the powerful name of Jesus. Allow the curse of occultism that has been allocated to waste my destiny to expire and be destroyed. Any blood crying out against me from any demonic altar, be quiet by Jesus' blood.

Then Lamech said to his wives: "Adah and Zillah, hear my voice; Wives of Lamech, listen to my speech! For I have killed a man for wounding me, Even a young man for hurting me. If Cain shall be avenged sevenfold, Then Lamech seventy-sevenfold."

So now you are cursed from the earth, which has opened its mouth to receive your brother's blood from your hand. When you till the ground, it shall no longer yield its strength to you. A fugitive and a vagabond you shall be on the earth."

(Genesis 4:23, 24, 11, 12)

In the name of Jesus, I command that every satanic wound in my life from my forefathers be healed completely. Father, Lord, release me from the demonic framework I inherited and set me free forever. Any blood-cry from my foundation, against my destiny, your time is up, shut your voice in Jesus' name. Every negative action performed against me by the occultic universe must be stopped right now. In the name of Jesus, Father, Lord, deliver me from every evil decision made to waste my destiny. Any unusual fire, sickness, or disease in any part of my life, I extinguish for good. In the name of Jesus, I command that any witchcraft resurgence going on against my life, both spiritually and physically, be put to an end. In the name of Jesus, expose and shame every opponent of my prosperity, settlement, and institution from the occult world. Every arrow of struggle, impatience, and defeat in my life has returned to its sender.

Because of the multitude of harlotries of the seductive harlot, The mistress of sorceries, Who sells nations through her harlotries, And families through her sorceries. (Nahum 3:4)

In the name of Jesus, stop any spiritual wars that are going on near my life. Stop any power from the dark world from taking away the good things in my life. Any strange noise, lie, whipping, or stealing will be put to an end by the blood of Jesus. In the name of Jesus, any witch or wizard who is working against me from the dark world should be shamed in public. In the name of Jesus, all-powerful God, use your power to help me with everything good. In the name of Jesus, all-powerful God, come to my aid and save me from the evil of the witchcraft kingdom.

DAY 3

Any power that is trying hard to keep me from my rights is a liar, and in the name of Jesus, I cut you out of my life. God's fire should destroy any plots, hate, or rejection that come from my base. In the name of Jesus, I pray that every evil plan that is being made to hurt my relationship with God will be found out and shamed. I give you back twice as much as the good things I and my family have lost to the devil.

But there was a certain man called Simon, who previously practiced sorcery in the city and astonished the people of Samaria, claiming that he was someone great, to whom they all gave heed, from the least to the greatest, saying, "This man is the great power of God." And they heeded him because he had astonished them with his sorceries for a long time. But when they believed Philip as he preached the things concerning the kingdom of God and the name of Jesus Christ, both men and women were baptized.

Acts 8:9-12

In the name of Jesus, I break free from my family, community witch, or wizard sent to waste me. In the name of Jesus, I command any mountain in front of me to vanish. Any witch or wizard that has control over my life must be revealed and shamed. Every witchcraft property in my body, catch fire and burn to ashes in the powerful name of Jesus. In the name of Jesus, any demonic personality utilizing sorcery against me be defeated. Almighty God, protect me from any witchcraft attacks. Any good door that has been closed against my destiny, be forced open in the name of Jesus. In the name of Jesus, I release myself from the clutches of witches and wizards. Any malevolent person who tries to manipulate my fate will fail miserably.

Now it happened, as we went to prayer, that a certain slave
girl possessed with a spirit of divination met us, who

brought her masters much profit by fortune-telling. This girl followed Paul and us, and cried out, saying, "These men are the servants of the Most High God, who proclaim to us the way of salvation." And this she did for many days. But Paul, greatly annoyed, turned and said to the spirit, "I command you in the name of Jesus Christ to come out of her." And he came out that very hour. But when her masters saw that their hope of profit was gone, they seized Paul and Silas and dragged them into the marketplace to the authorities. (Acts 16:16 19)

In the name of Jesus, I bind and cast out any witchcraft spirit within me. Any divination, magic, or sacrifice ever performed against me by anyone living or dead shall be extinguished in the name of Jesus. In the name of Jesus, I break and release myself from the yoke of witchcraft. In the name of Jesus, whatever part of my organ in any demonic altar, come out now.

Your Thank You Gift

As a token of gratitude for your purchase *Occult Grand Masters Exposed*, I am pleased to present you with both the book *"Commanding Your Dominion"* and the course *"Blueprint to Overcome Hatred & Rejection"* as a complimentary gift.

Please follow the link provided below, or enter the URL directly into your browser ↓

cojoseph.com

inted in Great Britain
by Amazon

₎50

ABOUT THE BOOK

Step into a realm few dare to tread with "Occult Grand Masters Exposed." This groundbreaking exposé uncovers the cryptic, often enigmatic practices of the Occult Kingdom, shedding light on the machinations of its Grand Masters. But this book is not merely a revelation—it's an arsenal.

Inside, you will discover:

The Veiled World: Dive deep into the intricacies of the Occult Kingdom, revealing the clandestine rituals, symbols, and agendas of its Grand Masters. Demystify the hidden mechanisms of Monitoring Spirits that have long been whispered about but rarely understood.

Armor Up: Arm yourself with potent spiritual warfare prayers and Dangerous Decrees to Destroy your Destroyers. Learn about Deliverance From Demonic Covenants And Curses, and become a spiritual sentinel, ever watchful and unyieldingly resistant to malevolent energies and demonic presence.

Tactical Insights: Gain strategic knowledge on breaking the chains and pulling down strongholds that occultic powers have established. This is not just about defense but mastering the art of spiritual offense using the weapons of our warfare.

Words as Weapons & The Power of Sacrifice: Discover the profound potency of spoken decrees—your verbal swords against darkness—and the Hidden Supernatural Power in Fasting and Prayer. Learn to voice them with precision, ensuring every occultic power in your path is halted dead in its tracks.

Venture forth equipped with knowledge and faith. Understand your opponent, bolster your defenses and step confidently into battle, knowing you possess the tools to ensure light conquers darkness ever

ABOUT THE AUTHOR

Joseph Okafor is a devoted pastor, Christian author, and Spiritual Warrior in the Lord's Vineyard. With a deep-rooted passion for spiritual warfare and deliverance, Joseph has dedicated his life to empowering believers in their journey of faith.

As a devoted servant of God, Joseph Okafor continues to serve in the Lord's Vineyard with unwavering dedication, committed to helping believers unlock their true potential, overcome the works of darkness, and live out their divine purpose.

Through his ministry, writings, and teachings, he stands as a guiding light, leading others to experience the transformative power of God's love and the victory found in Christ.

ISBN 9798860380950

90000

9 798860 380950